I0625461

Not Broken, Just Bent.

Written and Published by
Courtney Bygness

Preface

I'm the girl who buys poetry books to make it to
the other side of life's rough patches.
This time I decided to be the girl who wrote one
instead.
I hope you find meaning in the words that
healed me.
My heart has always had so much to say, I'm
ready to let it speak.

All my love, Courtney Bygness.

P.S. Poetry is written through blood, sweat and
tears. If you struggle with me through part one,
I promise it gets brighter.

Thank you for being here.

Not Broken, Just Bent.

Reminder: Brighter days are ahead. Keep choosing to turn the page, your story isn't over.

Part One: Dark

"Transparency"

growth is painful.
painful and raw.

"11:12"

I could feel forever
brushing it with my finger tips
but somewhere along the way
it wasn't enough

"What if's"

grieving what might have been
had you let me in
another time
another life
we could meet again

"Too bright"

you were the light to me
I wish I could have
returned the favor

"Sugarcoating it"

instead of reassurance
you could've given it to me straight
you can keep the chaser
I rather feel it burn

"Irony"

born with a healing heart
I'll heal yours
then I'll heal mine

"Tables that turned"

a book of mutual pages
a path so right
hooked a hard left
what could have been it
became what was

"Daydreaming"

hopes of a home together
now healing within the walls
of separate houses

"Decomposing"

I fell for you
ironically it was during fall
when leaves hit the ground
they rot
I will pick my heart up
before it gets the chance

"Voice of reason"

pain is loud.
listen to it.
absorb it.
grow from it.

"Changing of seasons"

winter came to steal
summer's glow
sooner than predicted

"A healing heart"

you showed me what heaven
must feel like
it was ripped away
as quickly as it came
when it ended it made me
want to go see
heaven for myself
my work down here is unfinished
our story might be too

"Empty expectations"

you cannot force people
to be who you
thought they were

"Had you known"

with a deadbolt on your heart
choose your words wisely
say less
do more

"Moving backwards"

to be friends with the one
I wanted to be old with
take my pride
is it better than goodbye?

"Shadows"

his demons danced in his darkness
telling him to run
when the light was too warm

"22nd St"

too much
too little
too late

"A dream"

too good to be true
so I pinched myself
now I'm missing you

"Simplify it"

tell me it was a lie
let me leave in the wind
tell me you didn't mean it
that you could've let me in

"The sun will rise"

I've seen what grief does to people
I've felt it within myself even
that's what keeps me here

"Battles with the night"

offering a shoulder to lean on
all while still craving
the broken parts of you

"Lonely soldier"

broken before we began
but I was prepared for the battle
you reminded me that some repairs
only require one

"Partly cloudy"

eyes that felt like refreshing rain
a mind that held the storm
a heart capable of so many depths

Part Two: Dusk

"Keep going"

a broken heart still beats
and for that I am grateful

"Welcome home"

the light is knocking
let it in
raise the shades once more
say goodbye to the darkness
it is not your friend

"Growing"

do the work
but do it for yourself

"Peace is priority"

peace is expensive
you will lose people
you will lose places
you will lose what you envisioned
do not lose yourself

"Don't turn cold"

nurture your heart
hear its needs
keep it warm

"The painter"

rock bottom is a clean canvas
change your perspective
make it a masterpiece

"No fault zone"

feelings are valid
do not water them down
you cannot keep something
that does not know how
to be kept

"Wait for them"

content hearts
and genuine smiles
they are on their way

"Next girl"

if she is handing you her heart
and you cannot provide for it
tell her

"Miscommunication"

I am okay
even if you cannot be
what you said you were

"It takes a woman"

I tried to be the woman
who saved you
only you can be the man
who saves himself

"A shattered season"

a moment
a memory
a second of sunshine
it was so bright
but the clouds wouldn't leave your mind

"Unsynced clocks"

everything I wanted
everything you needed
just not yet

"Next time I'll know"

I should not have assumed
the song you sang to me
was how you felt for me

"Trust fall"

let me down slowly
but call if you need
a pick me up

"Hard truth within grief"

they died
you did not
choose to live
it's the choice they don't have

"Opposites attract"

mr. hard to love
meets
ms. I can if you let me

"The best in you"

I showed you things
you didn't know were within you
I loved you for your darkness
but I knew there were
brighter things too

"Dear heartbreak"

it's been a while
you're never graceful
you demand my attention
please don't return
you can leave me in pieces
as long as you leave me alone

"Different equation, same conclusion"

you never wanted to break me
so you left
and the result was the same

"Coming home"

my heart isn't mine to give away
so I'll sit with myself
for a while
until she finds her way back to me

"The way we parted"

we left with grace
I'm still searching for my peace

"Lost and found"

as I found the good in you
I misplaced the good in me

"No contact: day one"

you will not have the chance
to miss me if
I am still there
but it's the only place
I want to be

"Frosted by grief"

blue eyes begging to be seen
as the winter creeps in
threatening to turn them to ice

"Another day"

the hardest battles aren't conquered
in one night
but if you wake to see the sunrise
it's a damn good place to start

Part Three: Dawn

"Choose to live"

do not let grief kill you
its taken enough already

"Not goodbye, but see you later"

do good in the world
be the light to those lost in the dark
and love the life you chose

"A warmth within fall"

we walked the same path
if only for a moment
a beautiful season was shared

"Undeniable"

permanency does not define
the depth it holds
within your heart

"Bittersweet"

love can be found in letting go

"You are deserving"

you will not be valued more
simply because you chose
to accept less

"Boundaries"

do not negotiate your worth

"Risk over regret"

there are countless ways to die
rejection is not one of them
life is too short
be afraid and do it anyways

"Architect"

it is up to you
to build the frame
for the life you picture

"Housekeeping"

healing is messy
but I would've cleaned
up after you

"By now"

by now he is who I
knew he could be

"The one that got away"

Come find me.

"Familiar"

it came with ease
as if our souls had already spoken
our hearts had danced in the past
the butterflies were welcoming
you home

"Who he is for you"

the dark days are less frequent
the mind isn't as messy
the heart has proven more capable
the words mirror the actions
do not take his self-improvement
for granted

"Get going"

put the past in your back pocket
pick up the pieces
dust them off
the lessons will help you
on your way

"A picture on the mantle"

silence lacking your laughter
weekends missing your wild
tomorrow arriving without you
peace on earth went with you

Dedicated to a good soul, gone way too soon.

"Work in progress"

I'm practicing the pronunciation
of, "no"
but every time I look at you
it comes out as yes

"Jigsaw"

the pieces never fit quite the same
I'm a different version
every time I'm whole again
but if you asked,
we could dump me out
and start from scratch

"Began and ended the same"

you caught my eye with manners
we parted with kindness

"One way ticket"

I traded my peace for
an adventure with a lost soul,
who puts on a solid act.
even if I had a free pass,
I wouldn't take the trip back.

"Back on track"

somewhere down the road
I'll be a better me
you'll be a better you
we can do this how
we were supposed to

"Unavailable"

the capacity to be
what I deserved
was out of stock.
I hope the shelves
get filled soon.

"Greener grass"

you water yours,
I'll water mine

"Radio silence"

storms come
and they go
I still want to tell you
they were here

"Loving from a distance"

the words come out as,
"see you later"
but I hope to see you around

"Practicing patience"

pondering what could have been,
what might still be.
how to get from here to there,
all while still in one piece.

"Substantial"

length is not a valid
measurement to determine
the impact a chapter
holds in your story

"My muse"

I hold gratitude
for experiencing an event
such as the way
our souls collided

Author's Note

If you made it to this page I truly could not hold
more appreciation for you.
Thank you for taking a chance on the words
within my heart.

Always remember, tomorrow will be as bright as
you let it be.
Sometimes in life, you have to step back and let
time do what time does.
It will always tell you all you need to know.

You all have my never ending gratitude.
I hope life treats you well.

Thank you, Courtney Bygness.